AFRICA

AFRICA

From the Nile Delta to Table Mountain

ANNE-MARIE BISSADA

amber
BOOKS

First published in 2023

Published by
Amber Books Ltd
United House
London N7 9DP
United Kingdom
www.amberbooks.co.uk
Instagram: amberbooksltd
Pinterest: amberbooksltd
Twitter: @amberbooks

ISBN: 978-1-83886-283-1

Project Editor: Michael Spilling
Designer: Keren Harragan
Picture Research: Terry Forshaw

Printed in China

Contents

Introduction

There is so much more to Africa than the usual images portrayed in everyday media. It's a continent alive with various cultures, languages, rituals, landscapes and colour. It's the different nuances from the hues of the Sahara where an oasis village pops out in its white splendour, to the lush greens of the rainforests where a lowland gorilla may be found. It's the pristine water that flows across the Zambezi River and spills into Victoria Falls, and the yearly flooding that brings out the crossing of the wildebeest in Kenya – truly one of the 'seven wonders of the natural world' – to the magical refuge hidden within the Lerai Forest inside Tanzania's Ngorongoro Crater. It's also the history that the continent has absorbed from its ancient civilizations to its numerous occupations. Take a walk on Gorée Island, meander the narrow streets of Lamu and Zanzibar's Stone Town or take in the colourful homes in Cape Town's Bo-Kaap neighbourhood. Marvel at the Great Zimbabwe Ruins, or the intricate rock-hewn churches in Ethiopia, or the wonders of the Pharaohs. No matter where you are, the blend of modern and past traditions is alive – this is Africa.

ABOVE:
The Sahara Desert at sunset.
OPPOSITE:
Zebras and wildebeest in the Ngorongoro
Crater, Tanzania.

North Africa

From towering sand dunes to pristine oases, the serenity and calm one finds in the middle of the desert are juxtaposed to the bustling medinas of Marrakesh, the labyrinth souq in Cairo and the grand boulevards of Algiers. This is North Africa, a region that spans from Morocco to Sudan.

Yet beneath all those bright turquoise waters, traditional sailing boats along the Nile River and sunsets in the desert are layers of history and hidden marvels. Visit the impressive architecture of Ghademes in Libya – known as the 'pearl of the desert' by the Berber – take in the natural splendour and mystery of Algeria's Rock Forests, marvel at the mysterious building of the Great Pyramids of Giza and Nubian pyramids in Sudan, and stroll down the large boulevards of Tunisia's Henri Bourgiba and Algier's Didouche Mourad, both renamed after their break from France.

Wade in the crystal blue waters off Tunisia's Soussa, scuba dive along the Red Sea Reef in South Sinai, sail down the Nile in a felucca or sample the fragrant cuisine of Morocco at its famed night markets, without forgetting to take in the impeccable Roman and Greek ruins in Libya. The region is a rich fabric woven from its numerous influences and geographic context.

OPPOSITE:
Abu al-Abbas al-Mursi Mosque, Alexandria, Egypt
Initially a mausoleum built in 1307 in honour of the 13th-century Spanish scholar and saint, Abu al-Abbas al-Mursi, his tomb became a place of pilgrimage for many Muslims. Today's structure dates back to 1775 after an Algerian sheikh built a large mosque on the site.

**Stanley Bridge,
Alexandria, Egypt**
Considered a landmark
in the city's Corniche
(boardwalk), this was the
first bridge in Egypt to be
constructed over the sea.
Completed in the 1990s, it
was built in an old Islamic
style to compliment the
royal Al-Montazah Palace,
the summer residence of
King Farouk.

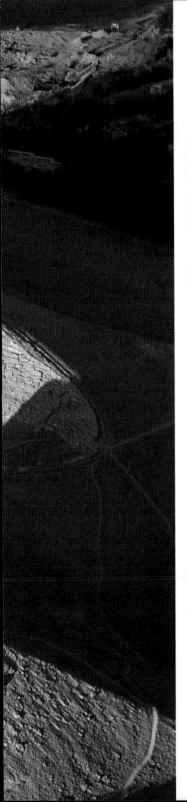

ALL PHOTOGRAPHS:
Abu Simbel, Aswan Governate, Egypt
The two massive rock-cut temples at Abu Simbel date to the 13th century BC. Following the creation of Lake Nasser during the construction of the Aswan High Dam in the 1960s, the original temple complex was cut and relocated to a higher man-made hill to prevent it being submerged by water.

Ras Mohammed National Park, Sharm El Sheikh, Sinai, Egypt
Egypt's first national park opened in 1983, shortly after the the country retook control of Sinai. Often considered to be the most stunning part of the peninsula, the park protects a small mangrove forest along with the Red Sea Reef – one of the world's most popular diving sites.

Beach in Sinai, Egypt, near Nuweiba
A sandy beach meets the Red Sea in Sinai Peninsula, near Nuweiba, a town on the eastern part of Sinai, close to the Gulf of Aqaba. Such picturesque landscapes dot the area known for its clear waters, mountains and small Bedouin villages.

Panorama of the Nile, from Cairo Tower, Egypt
One of Cairo's more modern monuments, the Cairo Tower
was once the tallest free-standing structure in Egypt when
built in 1971. Located on the island of Zamalek, it offers
the best view of the Nile looking south to Garden City
and Rhoda Island. Looking out to the Nile from the tower
just before sunset, the water is often dotted with feluccas
(traditional sailing boats).

RIGHT TOP:

Karnak Temple, Luxor, Egypt
The Karnak complex developed over a thousand years, mainly between the 12th and 20th dynasties, and involved nearly 30 pharaohs. Because of the many years taken to build Karnak, its final size, complexity and diversity is unparalleled.

RIGHT BOTTOM:

Healing sands, Aswan, Egypt
Aswan is renowned for the healing properties of its sands. The Aga Khan visited there when he suffered from rheumatism in 1954. After recovering from his illness, he built a small pink granite mausoleum on a hill above the area.

FAR RIGHT:

Great Hypostyle Hall, Temple of Amon Ra, Luxor, Egypt
Considered to be one of the greatest architectural marvels at Karnak is the hypostyle hall (a space with a roof supported by columns). It has 134 sandstone columns, with the centre 12 reaching 21m (69ft) in height. During its heyday, the hall's columns would have been colourfully painted.

Great Sphinx of Giza, Egypt
This monumental limestone statue with a human head and lion's body, may represent the pharaoh Khafre (2603–2578 BC). Known as the oldest monumental sculpture in Egypt, it measures 73m (240ft) long and 20m (66ft) high, and is thought to have been created during the Old Kingdom.

Giza Pyramids, Cairo, Egypt
One of the seven wonders of the world, the pyramids were built during the 4th dynasty of the Old Kingdom (2600–2500 BC). Pharaoh Khufu is believed to have started the pyramid project. There's much controversy about how these pyramids were built given that material had to be transported from quarries and then cut. Some theories point to the use of slave labour, whereas others suggest that of skilled Egyptian craftsmen.

OPPOSITE:
Muizz Street, Cairo, Egypt
Along this 1-km (0.6mi)
long street in old Fatimid
Cairo, one can find great
medieval architectural
treasures from the Islamic
era. Following extensive
government renovations to
the street and a ban on cars,
it has been converted into
an 'open-air museum'.

LEFT:
**Shop in Khan el-Khalili,
Cairo, Egypt**
The famous market in old
Cairo was initially a trade
centre during the Mamluk
period that continued to
grow as more merchants
built new shops, hence its
labyrinthine feel. Today it's
a major tourist attraction
where people come to buy
artisanal items.

LEFT:

Great Mosque of Mohammed Ali, Cairo, Egypt
Located within the citadel of old Cairo, this Ottoman mosque – commissioned by Mohammed Ali Pasha – was the largest to be built in the first half of the 19th century. Perched upon the summit of the citadel, it is a visible landmark across Cairo.

OPPOSITE:

Lake Qaroun, Fayoum Oasis, Egypt
This saltwater lake found within the Fayoum oasis is a designated protected area and is the remaining part of the ancient saltwater lake Moeris. Today Lake Qaroun is famed for its beauty and is home to thousands of migratory birds during the winter migration.

LEFT:

Suez Canal, Egypt
This artificial waterway was built in 1869 to connect the Mediterranean Sea to the Red Sea and to allow for quick travel between Europe and Asia. Attempts by the pharaohs to construct such a canal were never realized. In 2014, the government expanded one section to expedite travel time.

RIGHT:

Satellite shot, Suez Canal, Egypt
The Suez Canal stretches 193km (120mi) from Port Said in the north to Port Tewfik in the southern city of Suez. It cuts the sea voyage by 7000km (4350mi) between Europe and Asia.

Khartoum, Sudan
In the capital city of Khartoum the Blue and White Nile rivers merge to form the Nile that travels downstream to Egypt. Originally founded in 1821 as part of Ottoman Egypt, the city was later under British control.

University of Khartoum, Sudan
Considered the largest and oldest university in Sudan, the university was created by the British shortly after they gained power. Lord Kitchener proposed a college in memory of Gordon of Khartoum, who had been killed in battle. Its doors opened in 1902.

OPPOSITE:
Meroe pyramids, Kabushiya, Sudan
These Nubian pyramids were built during the Kushite Kingdom near the ancient city of Meroe to house three royal cemeteries. Today there are twice as many Nubian pyramids standing than there are in Egypt.

LEFT:

Decapitated statues, Cyrene, Libya

These statues standing in the ancient complex at Cyrene depict Demeter and Kore (Ceres and Persephone in Greek). The Greeks took over the city in 630 BC and transformed it into the largest and wealthiest Greek colony in North Africa. The grounds extend over 32km (20mi) and include a temple and theatre complex.

RIGHT:

Theatre at Leptis Magna ruins, near Khoms, Libya

Leptis Magna, once a major city and port founded by the Carthaginian Empire in the 7th century BC, grew under the Romans. The theatre was built around AD 56 in an ancient quarry. It is revered for being well-preserved, given it remained buried beneath sand for centuries.

ALL PHOTOGRAPHS:
Ghademes, Libya
Considered to be the 'pearl of the desert' by the Berber for its white buildings in the middle of the desert, Ghademes is one of the oldest pre-Saharan cities. Its centre is a labyrinth of 1300 mud-brick homes with connecting roofs.

ALL PHOTOGRAPHS:
Art treasures, Leptis Magna, Libya
The ancient Carthaginian city of Leptis Magna was incorporated into the Roman Province and became a major trading hub with the rest of the Mediterranean. It was one of the most beautiful cities of the Roman Empire with its intricate artwork and lavish monuments. A detail of a Roman floor mosaic features a chariot being pulled by leopards (left).

**Didouche Mourad Street,
Algiers, Algeria**
Considered to be one of the
most beautiful streets in
Algiers, Didouche Mourad
was called Rue Michelet
under the French. It was
famous for its luxurious
shops and dynamic
ambience. Following
independence, the street was
renamed after a hero of the
Algerian War.

OPPOSITE:
**Our Lady of Africa Basilica,
Algiers, Algeria**
Completed in 1872
following 14 years of
construction, this basilica
is located on the north side
of Algiers. It's the sister
church to France's Notre-
Dame de la Garde basilica
in Marseilles.

Kasbah in Algiers, Algeria
The traditional walled citadel of Algiers was founded on the ruins of 10th-century Icosium. Divided into a 'high city' and a 'low city', it houses many old mosques from the 17th century. The citadel played an important role in insurgency planning during the war of independence.

Martyrs' Memorial, Algiers, Algeria
Inaugurated on the 20th anniversary of the Algerian War, the concrete structure is built in the shape of three palm leaves. Beneath where the leaves join is the 'Eternal Flame' that commemorates the lives lost in the struggle for independence.

RIGHT TOP:

Umm al-Ma'a Lake, Ubari Desert, south-west Libya
Known as the Ubari Sand Sea, the desert is home to 20 saline lakes. Umm al-Ma'a (Mother of Water in Arabic) is one of the most beautiful lakes in the region.

RIGHT BOTTOM:

Tassili N'Ajjer National Park, Sahara Desert, Algeria
The vast national park covers 72,000sq km (27,800sq mi) of the Sahara Desert. Rolling sand dunes eventually open into what are known as 'rock forests' that feature otherworldly sandstone rock formations created by erosion.

FAR RIGHT:

Camel caravan, Sahara Desert
The Sahara is the largest hot desert in the world. The domestication of camels in the 3rd century allowed the Berber to move easily across the desert, but regular trade routes developed under the spread of Islam in the 7th and 8th centuries.

42

**Outdoor street food market,
Jemaa el-Fnaa, Marrakesh,
Morocco**
Located in the old medina,
this is a gathering place for
tourists and locals alike.
During the day, it's packed
with fresh orange juice
sellers and snake charmers,
and at night, food stalls and
tents go up and the air fills
with the aroma of spices
and cooking.

OPPOSITE:
**Chouara tannery,
Fes, Morocco**
One of the largest and
oldest of the three tanneries
in the old city of Fes that
continues to operate in the
same traditional way since
its foundation. Although its
exact age is unknown, it has
remained an integral part of
the city's economy.

Hammamet, Tunisia
A typical house found
within the narrow streets
in the old medina of the
seaside city of Hammamet
('baths' in Arabic).
Originally a Roman
colony in the 2nd century,
Hammamet is known
today for its beaches,
amphitheatre and jasmine.

OPPOSITE (BOTH PHOTOGRAPHS):
El Jem, Tunisia
Called Thysdrus by the
Romans, El Jem was one of
the most important towns in
North Africa after Carthage.
It remains a hub of olive oil
production. Its 3rd-century
amphitheatre, which was
built similarly to Rome's
Coliseum, held up to 35,000
people making it one of the
largest in the world.

LEFT:

Ribat of Soussa, Tunisia
The 8th-century ribat (fortress) is the oldest one in Tunisia. Built by Ibrahim the Great, its initial modest structure was revamped under Ziyadat Allah I in 821.

ABOVE:

Soussa, Tunisia
Visiting Soussa allows one to meander through its medieval medina of narrow streets, as well as easily access some of the finest beaches from the city centre.

ABOVE AND LEFT:
Troglodyte house, Matmata, Tunisia
These traditional cave houses have been in existence since Phoenician times to allow residents to protect themselves from severe heat. Matmata, a small Berber town in southern Tunisia, is prone to heatwaves. The photograph (left) shows an interior of a cave house in Matmata.

FAR LEFT:
Avenue Habib Bourguiba, Tunis, Tunisia
Named after Habib Bourguiba, the first President of Tunisia post-independence, this tree-lined avenue in central Tunis connects the old medina with the new Tunis through its wide boulevard, which has been compared to Paris's Champs Elysées.

51

West Africa

From Benin's magical Ganvié village – built entirely on stilts in the middle of a lake to keep away slave catchers – to the impressively tall, entirely mud-brick Grand Mosque in Niger's historic city of Agadez, West Africa is a intriguing region in which the ancient past exists in harmony with the present.

The Sahara Desert has strongly influenced the region from the sun-baked, adobe and mud-brick architecture of Mali to the impact of the trans-Saharan trade route on northern Nigeria's Kano city. West Africa's coast was also the epicentre of the transatlantic slave trade, which left its mark on the many colonial-style towns that have turned themselves into havens of peace. Gorée Island, once the largest slave-trading centre on the coast is now a beacon of serenity away from the chaos of the Senegalese capital and a pilgrimage destination for the African diaspora.

Today, the countries of West Africa revel in the natural beauty that surrounds them, from the Sindou Peaks of Burkina Faso to the Bandiagara Cliffs in Mali, which hold a special place for the Dogon people. Visitors can enjoy the picture-perfect beaches of Guinea and Nigeria's Lekki, and marvel at the African bush elephants strolling through Ghana's outstanding Mole National Park.

OPPOSITE:
Boats collecting salt, Lake Retba, Senegal
Named for its pink waters caused by the *Dunaliella salina* algae, the high salt content of this lake is comparable to that of Israel's Dead Sea. Few organisms survive in Lake Retba's salty waters, however, many locals harvest the salt that is mainly used for preserving fish.

Street on Gorée Island, Senegal
Despite its grim history, present-day Gorée is a place of peace and lush beauty. The no-car island is a quiet haven with its narrow cobblestone streets and old colonial buildings still wearing their pastel colours.

Aerial view of Gorée, Senegal
An aerial shot of the small island shows the former slave fortress. One of the oldest sites of European settlement on the African coast, Gorée was the largest slave-trading centre from the 15th to 19th century. It was the final stop for slaves before they were transported over to the Americas.

RIGHT:

Storing huts in Joal-Fadiouth, Senegal

The town is essentially two communities: Joal on the mainland and Fadiouth on an island. The two are connected by bridge. Residents traditionally stored their grains in huts placed high on stilts to protect them from insects and the high tide.

OPPOSITE:

Mangrove forest, Sine-Saloum Delta, Joal-Fadiouth, Senegal

Aerial view of a mangrove forest in the Sine-Saloum Delta where the rivers converge as they flow into the Atlantic Ocean. Due to the slow waterflow, the delta remains salty, which makes it a prime habitat for mangroves.

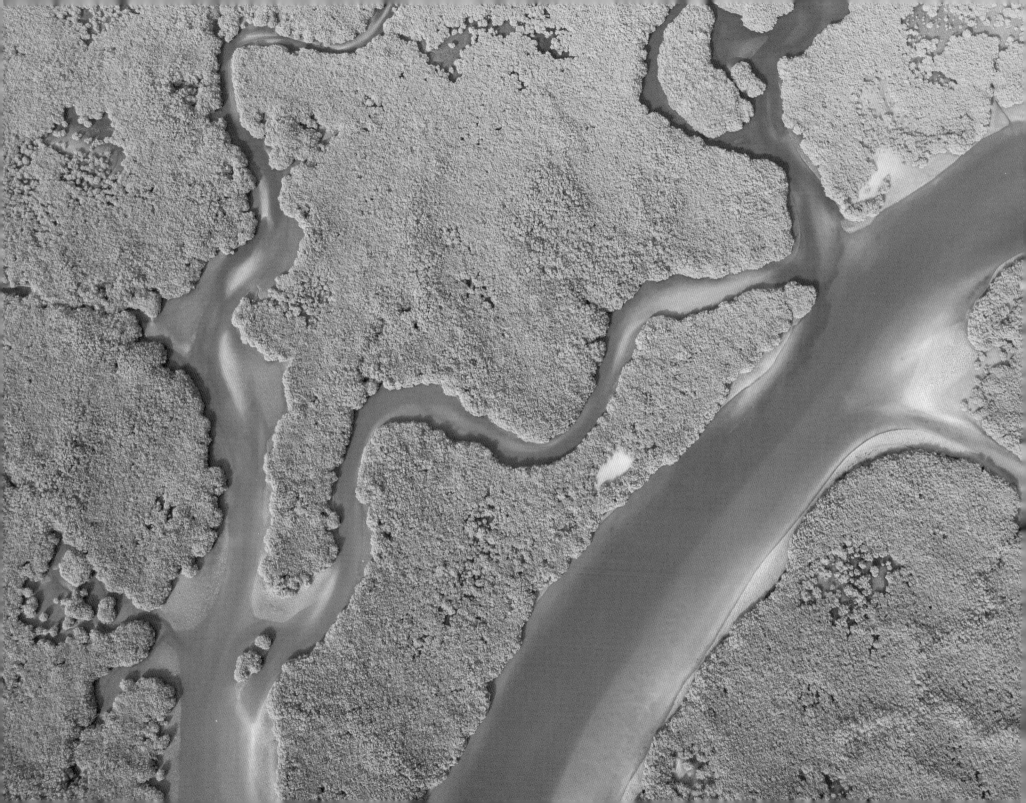

RIGHT:

Fishing port of Ponta do Sol village, Santo Antão, Cape Verde

Ponta do Sol is one of the oldest settlements in the southern Cape Verde islands. Fishing remains crucial in this charming village and its colourful fishing boats head out to sea daily.

OPPOSITE:

Praia Street workshop, Mindelo, São Vicente, Cape Verde

The port city of Mindelo is the cultural capital of Cape Verde, particularly known for its music and art. Manuel and Tchalé Figueira are internationally renowned painters who live in Mindelo.

Waterfall, Guinea
Waterfalls are one of
Guinea's many attractions.
This one is described as
'bridal veil' due to its
dramatic, veil-like torrent of
water. The best time to enjoy
its beauty is during the rainy
season, between August and
September.

**Red gravel road, Fouta-
Djallon, Guinea**
The heavy rainfall in this
highland region has led to its
nickname of 'the water tower
of West Africa'. The region's
gravel roads owes their red
hue to the high concentration
of bauxite deposits.

**Bel-Air Beach,
Guinea-Conakry**
Bel-Air is one of the most
breathtaking beaches in
Guinea. This small remote
beach has white sand lined
with palm trees and calm
turquoise waters, making it
a favourite among locals and
tourists.

Post and Customs building, Grand-Bassam, Côte d'Ivoire

Grand-Bassam was the French colonial capital of Côte d'Ivoire. Today it's divided into two: Old Bassam, with the faded grandeur of its colonial architecture such as the old Post and Customs, and New Bassam, the commercial centre, which was once the African servants' quarters.

RIGHT:

Street market, Abidjan, Côte d'Ivoire

All over the capital city of Abidjan, there are busy open-air markets selling seasonal fruits and vegetables such as cassava, a root vegetable used to make the popular side dish *attiéké*.

Elmina Castle, Ghana
This whitewashed castle was the first trading post on the Gulf of Guinea and is the oldest European building in sub-Saharan Africa. Built by the Portuguese in 1482, it was later conquered by the Dutch. Gold exports were replaced by human chattel during the transatlantic slave trade. The castle housed bsaement dungeons where slaves were kept before they were shipped off to the Americas, after passing through the 'door of no return'.

Nzulezu stilt village, Lake Tadane, Ghana
This 400-year-old coastal village in western Ghana was
entirely built on stilt-supported platforms over Lake Tadane.
It may have been built over water for protection during tribal
attacks and can only be reached by canoe. The village has only
recently opened up to tourists.

ABOVE:
Herd of kob, Mole National Park, Ghana
The kob is a type of antelope normally found in wet areas in
West Africa. They live in small herds but can join larger groups
of up to 1000 animals. This herd live in Mole National Park,
Ghana's largest protected wildlife areas.

RIGHT:

African elephant, Mole National Park, Ghana

There are two types of African elephants: the African bush and the smaller African forest. Both are social herbivores that are under a high threat of extinction.

FAR RIGHT:

Kakum National Park, Ghana

The rival to Mole National Park, Kakum National Park encompasses thick tropical forests and is known for its series of hanging rope bridges. From the Kakum Canopy Walkway visitors can observe the wildlife from a normally inaccessible vantage point.

LEFT:

Cape Coast, Ghana
Considered one of the country's most historic cities, this busy fishing port was originally called Oguaa (meaning 'river of crabs') before the arrival of the Portuguese in 1471. It's famed for its vibrant festivals, hosting some 32 annually, in particular Fetu Afahye, which is held in early September.

OPPOSITE:

Black Star Gate, Accra, Ghana
This monument is one of three structures in Independence Square commissioned by Kwame Nkrumah, the first President of Ghana following independence from Britain in 1957. The five-point black star represents Africa in general and Ghana in particular, and bears the inscription 'AD 1957' and 'Freedom and Justice.'

LEFT:
Grand Mosque of Bobo-Dioulasso, Burkina Faso
Constructed from clay and wooden beams that protrude on the exterior, the mosque was built between 1812 and 1823. The area was once ruled by the Kingdom of Sia; when it faced attack, a local Islamic religious leader offered aid on the condition that the king build a mosque.

RIGHT:
Market, Ouagadougou, Burkina Faso
The Burkinabé capital – often shortened to Ouaga – boasts many bustling street markets where it is possible to buy locally grown fruit and vegetables.

ABOVE:

Monument of National Heroes, Ouagadougou, Burkina Faso
This eye-catching monument commemorates Burkina's
independence from France in 1960. It features two gourds,
one upside down at the base and the other on top; the four
supporting 'legs' represent the stages of the people's struggle:
independence, republic, revolution and democracy.

RIGHT:

Sindou Peaks, Burkina Faso
Considered to be one of the country's most unforgettable
sights, these craggy geological sandstone formations were
underwater millions of years ago. Many hikers come here to
climb Mount Tenakourou, the highest peak in Burkina Faso.

Great Mosque of Djenné, Mali

Located in the city of Djenné in northern Mali, the first mosque was built in the 13th century, but the current structure dates from 1907. The walls are made of sun-baked earth bricks that are coated with plaster, which gives the building its smooth, sculpted appearance (far right). The walls are distinctively studded with bundles of palm trunk (called toron) that stick out about 60cm (23in), allowing them to be used as scaffolding during annual repairs.

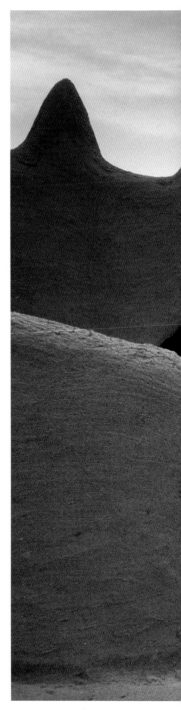

LEFT & OPPOSITE:

Bandiagara Cliff, Mali
This dramatic sandstone cliff rises to about 500m (1640ft). Traditionally this is the land of the cliff-dwelling Dogon people, but before them the area was inhabited by the Tellem and Toloy. Many structures from the Tellem remain today, such as caves carved into the cliffs (left).

FAR LEFT:

Dogon dancers, Bandiagara Cliff, Mali
The Dogon perform this dance on stilts every 50 to 60 years. The ritual, which can take years to complete, represents a handover of secrets from the older generation to the next. Masked men wear 3-m (10ft) long stilts and perform a religious dance ceremony known as *sigui*.

Eco-friendly architecture, Djenné, Mali
The adobe buildings in Mali are considered among some of the finest examples of architecture using local materials, raw earth known locally as *banco*. However, modern construction methods pose a threat to this eco-friendly architecture.

OPPOSITE:
Saba Mosque, Mali
The unique design of West Africa's adobe mosques are well-suited to the region's very hot climate. Saba's mosque was built from sundried bricks made of clay, mud, sand and water mixed with binding straw. With timber a rare and costly commodity, palm wood is used sparingly in the roof and scaffolding built into the structure for the workers who apply plaster annually. Walls are thick and tapered to protect the inside from heat and support upper levels, whereas vents allow for light and air to circulate and keep the interior cool.

**'Venice of Africa',
Ganvié village, Benin**
Built on Lake Nokoué around
400 years ago, this village on
stilts was borne out of slavery.
To escape soldiers from the
Fon tribe who sold people to
the Portugese, the Tonfinu
took refuge at this lake,
knowing that the Fon feared a
demon who lived underwater.
Ganvié means 'we survived'
in the local language.

RIGHT:

**Ganvié, Lake Nokoué,
Benin**
Three thousand buildings
are spread out across this
lakeside village-on-stilts in
southern Benin. The primary
way to make a living is
fishing. Everything in Ganvié
is accessed via narrow boats,
or pirogues, the only form
of transportation.

RIGHT:
Traditional bakery, Agadez, Niger
The interior of an old bakery in Agadez, a desert city that grew by being at the crossroads of trans-Saharan trade. It was founded before the 14th century and eventually became an important city of the semi-nomadic Tuareg people. Caravans still arrive at the city bringing valuable salt from Bilma.

OPPOSITE TOP & BOTTOM:
Grand Mosque, Agadez, Niger
Entirely constructed from clay, and built in 1515, the Grand Mosque is considered to be the tallest mud-brick structure in the world. Its minaret stands 27m (88ft) high.

LEFT:

Spices for sale at a market, Kano, Nigeria

The city of Kano in northern Nigeria is a major route of the trans-Saharan trade. Islam arrived in the city in the 11th century via trans-Saharan trade and transformed the city into a wealthy and commercial centre known for its leather and cotton goods.

OPPOSITE LEFT:

Great Mosque of Kano, Kano, Nigeria

The original 15th-century mud mosque resulted from a collaboration between Sarken Muhammed Ruma and Egyptian 'Abd al-Rahman. Reconstructed in the 1950s, it remains one of the oldest mosques in Nigeria.

OPPOSITE RIGHT:

Kano, seen from Dala Hill, Nigeria

The capital of Kano State, Kano has a population of around 3.6 million, which gives it a busy bustling atmosphere. Situated at a crossroads of historic trading routes, there has been a settlement here for more than a thousand years.

RIGHT:

Lekki Beach, Lagos, Nigeria
Situated in the island city of Lagos, Eleko or Lekki Beach is on a naturally formed peninsula connected to Lagos. With its beautiful beaches, it is home to some of the most expensive real estate in Lagos.

OPPOSITE LEFT:

Canopy walkway, Lekki, Lagos, Nigeria
At the Lekki Conservation Centre this suspended walkway rises over the reserve. It is the longest of its type in Africa and features six towers from where it's possible to watch monkeys, crocodiles and birds among other wildlife.

OPPOSITE RIGHT:

Lekki Conservation Centre, Lagos, Nigeria
Founded in 1990, the Conservation Centre was created as a sanctuary on Lekki Peninsula to protect wildlife, flora and fauna in the south-west coastal region against the backdrop of massive urban development.

LEFT:

Victoria Island, Lagos, Nigeria

An affluent area in Lagos, this is the main business and financial centre of Lagos. The island was originally surrounded by water, but under the British, the eastern swamps were filled to reduce mosquito breeding areas, thereby creating a land bridge to Lekki Peninsula.

OPPOSITE:

Balogun market, Lagos, Nigeria

The largest market in Lagos, Balogun is spread out over many streets on Lagos Island. It is known as one of the best markets to buy textiles and fashion accessories.

Central Africa

In Central Africa it is possible to encounter a range of extremes. Here you can follow the path of the powerful Congo River – the deepest in the world –get lost in Gabon's Loango National Park – once described as Africa's 'Last Eden' – or climb the highest point in Cameroon at Mount Fako.

Here too visitors can explore the rock formations in the Ennedi Plateau in Chad, take in the prehistoric rock art inside the Manda Guéli Cave or come across a lowland gorilla or forest elephant while roaming the rainforests of Gabon. The region is also home to the only active volcanoes in Africa in the Democratic Republic of Congo, and to the world's second-largest tropical rainforest in the Congo Basin. But don't forget to take a moment to explore the pristine waters surrounding Inhame beach at São Tomé and Príncipe.

Behind all that natural beauty lies the rich, multilayered history of ancient civilizations whose traditions have been kept alive despite the ever-changing dynamics on the continent. There is much to discover and experience – from the initiation ceremony of the Mbuti boys in the Ituri Forest and the sheep herder in the Chadian countryside who continues the semi-nomadic life of his ancestors to the mesmerizing vocal music of the Baka in the Central African Republic.

OPPOSITE:
Guelta d'Archei waterhole, Ennedi Plateau, Chad
This guelta, or desert pond, is one of the most famous examples in the Sahara. Several types of animal live here, notably the West African crocodile.

**Rock formations,
Ennedi plateau, Chad**
The Ennedi plateau is part
of the group of mountains
known as the Ennedi Massif.
The plateau is a sandstone
structure that spans across
the middle of the Sahara. Its
present-day shapes come from
exposure to sand and wind.

OPPOSITE:
Ennedi caves, Chad
Within the Ennedi mountains
in the Manda Guéli Cave,
an extensive collection of
prehistoric rock art dating
back 7000 years ago depicts
both humans and animals
including cattle.

Sheep herder, Chad
Sheep farming is of particular importance to Sahel countries given it allows a family to survive in a region defined by its desert climate. However, increasing environmental pressures such as desertification and soil degradation are making it difficult for these semi-nomadic pastoralists to survive.

ALL PHOTOGRAPHS:
**Boali Falls on the Mbali (M'Bari) River,
Central African Republic**
One of the best-known landmarks in the Central African
Republic, Boali town is revered for its nearby waterfalls.
They are most impressive during the rainy season when they
boom with water.

ABOVE:
Mount Cameroon, Cameroon
This active volcano in the south-west region of Cameroon is also known as Mount Fako. Its indigenous name, Mongo ma Ndemi, means 'Mountain of Greatness'. It is the highest point in sub-Saharan West and Central Africa.

RIGHT:
Craters at Mount Cameroon, Cameroon
Part of the Cameroon Volcanic Line, the mountain is one of the most active volcanoes in Africa and has erupted seven times in the last hundred years. In 2000, Mount Cameroon erupted producing explosions from two different craters.

RIGHT:

Rattan palm, Loango National Park, Gabon

Loango is justifiably referred to as Africa's Last Eden as much of it remains untouched and protected, including rattan – a climbing palm.

OPPOSITE:

Lowland gorilla, Loango National Park, Gabon

The national park is home to nearly 1500 western lowland gorillas, about 20 per cent of the country's endangered gorilla population. Many are threatened through poaching, disease and loss of habitat. Eco-tourism is one way to protect the population.

103

ABOVE:

Akaka Forest Camp, Loango National Park, Gabon
Located on the Rembo Ngowe River, these tropical wetlands are lined with lush and dense forest where elephants, red mangabeys, buffalos and other smaller mammals live.

RIGHT:

Forest elephants, Loango National Park, Gabon
There are two types of African elephants: forest and savanna. Both are in decline to due to habitat loss, poaching and human contact. Gabon is home to nearly 80 per cent of the world's forest elephants.

LEFT:

Women washing clothes in a riverbed, São Tomé and Príncipe
Those who live near rivers and streams use them to wash clothes and to bathe in. Women usually visit the streams after the hottest part of the day.

OPPOSITE:

São Sebastião Museum Fortress, São Tomé city, São Tomé and Príncipe
The 16th-century fortress was built by the Portuguese in 1566 to protect the port and the city against pirate attacks. It is now a museum containing religious art and colonial-era artefacts.

ABOVE:
Mercado Grande, São Tomé city, São Tomé and Príncipe
A main market in the city, Mercado Grande is divided into two
large halls beside each other: Mercado Municipal (municipal
market) and Mercado Novo (new market). The municipal
market (above) is chaotic, dynamic and noisy whereas Novo
is calmer and more organized.

RIGHT:
Old colonial building, São Tomé city
Established in the 15th century by Portugal, São Tomé is one
of Africa's oldest colonial cities. The islands were uninhabited
until their discovery by the Portuguese who then used them as
a trading centre for the trans-Atlantic slave trade.

**Inhame beach,
São Tomé and Príncipe**
At the southernmost part
of São Tomé, there is very
little around apart from
Praia Inhame Eco-lodge
close to one of the island's
finest beaches.

Mbuti boys, Ituri rainforest, Democratic Republic of Congo

These boys belong to the pygmy hunter-gathering Mbuti people. Decorated with traditional blue body paint and wearing straw skirts, they make their way to the forest to undergo an initiation ceremony called *nkumbi* – a coming-of-age ritual that involves circumcision.

Baka performing music, Grand Batanga, Cameroon

Music and dance remains central to the Baka people. Traditionally the women sing while the men dance. The Baka are native to the south-eastern rainforests of Cameroon, the northern Republic of Congo, northern Gabon, and south-western Central African Republic.

RIGHT:

Nyiragongo and Nyamuragira volcanoes, Virunga National Park, DR Congo

Both are active, but Nyamuragira is the most active volcano in Africa. Nyiragongo's most recent erupted in 2021. The two volcanoes sit in the Virunga National Park, which has a unique biodiversity owing to the volcanic activity.

OPPOSITE:

Silverback Mountain gorilla, Virunga National Park, DR Congo

One-third of the world's estimated remaining gorillas live in the national park. Unlike their lowland cousins, mountain gorillas have thick hair, an evolutionary adaptation to protect them in sub-zero temperatures in the higher altitudes.

LEFT TOP:
Mount Nyiragongo, DR Congo
A burning lava lake on Mount Nyiragongo at night.

LEFT BOTTOM:
Mount Nyiragongo, Virunga National Park, DR Congo
Aerial view of the active volcano Mount Nyiragongo in the Virunga Mountains.

RIGHT:
Farmers' fields beneath Mount Nyiragongo, DR Congo
Due to the volcanic eruptions, soil in the area is particularly fertile. However, following an eruption, such as the latest in 2018, farmers are forced to start again from scratch.

OVERLEAF:
Congo rainforest
The Congo rainforest is the world's second largest (after the Amazon) and is revered for its high level of biodiversity. It includes more than 600 tree species and 10,000 animal species, such as leopards, hippos and lions. The rainforest extends across the basin of the Congo River and its tributaries. It is the only major rainforest that absorbs more carbon than it emits.

Houses built on stilts, Congo River, DR Congo
Along the Congo River, buildings are often constructed on stilts to better withstand tropical storms and flooding in areas prone to high tides.

LEFT:
Boats berth at the Congo River crossing, Kisangani, DR Congo
Kisangani is the provincial capital of Tshopo, long considered the commercial capital of northern Congo. It is the country's most important inland port and the last navigable part on the Congo.

ABOVE:
Tropical rainforest, DR Congo
Around 65 per cent of the Republic of Congo is covered by rainforest, but the larger portion of the Congolese rainforest is found in Democratic Republic of Congo. The Congo is the deepest river in the world and the second largest in Africa.

RIGHT TOP:

Johnston's three-horned chameleon, Kahuzi-Biega National Park, DR Congo

This chameleon is native to the Albertine Rift in Central Africa, and is named after the British explorer Harry Johnston. The male possesses three brown horns, one on the nose and one above each eye. Females have no horns.

RIGHT BOTTOM:

Olive baboon, Kahuzi-Biega National Park, DR Congo

This adult baboon is native to 25 countries across Africa. Its name refers not to any olives it may eat, but to the colour of its fur.

FAR RIGHT:

Bridge at Djoué River, Republic of Congo

The crossing at Djoué has always been riddled with obstacles and was traditionally made using pirogues, a type of canoe. As more cars entered Congo, a solution had to be found. First a wooden bridge, then this concrete one was built in 1931–32.

124

LEFT:

Nabemba Tower, Brazzaville, Republic of Congo

This high-rise office block is the tallest building in the country. Damaged during the civil war, the cost to fix it was more than its initial price, and its yearly maintenance fees remain exorbitant. Many regard it more as a symbol of prestige than a necessity on the Brazzaville skyline.

RIGHT:

Grand Mosque, Brazzaville, Republic of Congo

About 2 per cent of the population in Republic of Congo is Muslim. This mosque was built in 2005 by the many immigrants from across North and West Africa, as well as Lebanon.

OPPOSITE:

Brazzaville, Republic of Congo

The capital and largest city of the Congo Republic, it is located on the north side of the Congo River, opposite Kinshasa, the capital of its neighbour DR Congo.

East Africa

From a colourful 6th-century monastery perched high in the Tigrayan mountains of north Ethiopia to the pristine beaches of Zanzibar and Lamu, East Africa is teeming with colour and history. Climb a 300-m (980ft) cliff to reach Ethiopia's Abuna Yemata Guh Church to feel 'closer to God', as the locals say, or witness one of the seven wonders of the natural world at the start of the rainy season when the wildebeest make their perilous migratory journey from Tanzania to Masai Mara National Reserve in south-west Kenya.

A wander through the spice markets of Zanzibar's Stone Town will stimulate your senses and take you back centuries. Or sit back and listen to the fishermen sing on the waters of Lake Kivu. Feel the sheer energy of one of the world's most powerful waterfalls at Murchison Falls in Uganda and admire the unforgettable sight at Ngorongoro Crater in the Great Rift Valley where the magical Lerai Forest is home to some 25,000 mammals, including the densest population of lions.

No one may be able to explain the origin of the name Kilimanjaro, but it's well worth climbing the highest single, free-standing mountain in the world in Tanzania. And don't forget to take time to marvel at the wonders of nature at Lake Bogoria, Kenya, whose waters attract some of the world's largest populations of striking flamingos.

OPPOSITE:
Debre Damo Monastery, Tigray region, Ethiopia
Debre Damo is a 6th-century monastery that sits atop a mountain. It is accessible only by rope up a 15-m (50ft) high cliff. Intrepid visitors tie a plaited leather rope around their waists and are pulled up by a monk at the top of the cliff.

LEFT:

Abuna Yemata Guh church, Tigray, Ethiopia

One of 35 rock-hewn churches in northern Ethiopia, the 6th-century church of Abuna Yemata Guh is located within a spectacular landscape, and requires a 45-minute climb up a sheer cliff and crossing narrow ledges to visit it.

RIGHT & FAR RIGHT:

Wall paintings, Abuna Yemata Guh church, Ethiopia

'From this rock, we are closer to God' is what many Ethiopians say after climbing to get to this 'church in the sky'. Inside, well-preserved 15th-century frescoes on the roof and walls depict angels and apostles, watched over by a priest of the Ethiopian Orthodox Church.

Mursi woman wearing a lip plate, Omo Valley, Ethiopia
The Mursi people live in south-west Ethiopia where they continue many traditional practices. Large clay plates are worn by women in their lower lip. The custom is linked to a woman's fertility and eligibility for marriage.

FAR LEFT:
Dassanech village, Omo River, Ethiopia
The Dassanech are a primarily agropastoral people who have adapted to living in extreme conditions. Their dome-shaped huts are made by weaving branches that are then covered with animal skins during the rainy season, and straw and leaves during the dry season.

RIGHT:

Mursi boys walking on stilts, Omo Valley, Ethiopia

The Mursi boys and men paint their bodies using clay and minerals from the earth for two reasons: to ward off evil spirits and to attract the opposite sex. The clay also serves as a type of sunscreen and insect repellent.

OPPOSITE:

Dassanech children holding animals, Omo River, Ethiopia

The Dassanech are an agropastoral people who have adapted to living in extreme conditions. The dome shaped huts are made by weaving branches that are then covered with animal skins during the rainy season, and straw and leaves during the dry season.

Saint George Church, Lalibela, Ethiopia
One of the 11 rock-hewn churches in Lalibela, Saint George (known locally as Bete Gyorgis) is considered the most iconic due to its cross shape. It dates from the early 12th or 13th century. The churches were built by Lalibela, King of Ethiopia, to create a 'new Jerusalem'.

Timket festival, Saint George Church, Lalibela, Ethiopia
One of the most important feast days on the Ethiopian orthodox calendar, these three days starting on 19 January are dedicated to celebrating the epiphany of Jesus Christ. The festival includes communal baptisms.

ABOVE:

Golden Monkey, Mgahinga Gorilla National Park, Uganda
This monkey – named for its bright gold-orange body – is one
of Uganda's 20 primate species found in highland forests of
the Virunga volcanic region. Due to the growing destruction
of their habitat, they are a seriously endangered species.

RIGHT:

Murchison Falls National Park (MFNP), Uganda
This is considered one of the world's most powerful waterfalls
where the Nile River forces its way through a gap in the rocks
that is only 7m (23ft) wide and then drops 45m (147ft). MFNP
is Uganda's largest national park.

**Giraffes, Masai
Mara National Reserve,
Kenya**
Also known as Kilimanjaro
giraffes, Masai giraffes are
the tallest living land animals.
Unlike reticulated (Somali)
giraffes, their bodies have
jagged irregular spots. The
rolling savanna plains of the
Masai Mara contain unique
wildlife conservation, making
it exceptional for safari tours.

Wildebeest crossing the Mara River, Masai Mara National Reserve, Kenya
Every year at the start of the rainy season, over a million wildebeest make the dangerous crossing from Tanzania to the Masai Mara in search of grazing and water. The Great Migration is the largest overland migration in the world.

African cheetahs, Masai Mara National Reserve, Kenya
The national reserve is a prime place to see cheetahs in their natural habitat. The bodies of these graceful and powerful cats are built for sheer speed, making them the fastest land mammal on earth at 110km/h (70mph). Cheetahs are classed as a critically endangered species.

ALL PHOTOGRAPHS:
Lamu Island, Kenya
The port city and island of
Lamu was founded in the
12th century. Built from coral
stone and mangrove timber,
the town is known for its
simple structures enhanced
by inner courtyards, verandas
and elaborately carved
wooden doors. The town's
winding narrow roads mean
residents either walk or use
donkeys to get around as cars
are banned.

Lamu old town waterfront, Kenya
Unlike other Swahili settlements in the area that have been abandoned, Lamu has continuously been inhabited for over 700 years. In the 14th century, a port was built on the island by Arab traders, which allowed the island to prosper during the East African slave trade. The influences from Arabia, Persia, India and Europe over the centuries has created a distinct culture.

Fishing dhows, Lamu Island, Kenya
Once the largest traditional boats of the Indian Ocean, these wooden sailboats were used to transport exotic spices and goods between East Africa, Asia and the Arabian Peninsula.

RIGHT:

White Rhino, Solio Ranch (Solio Reserve), Kenya

Named after Solio, a great Masai chief, the privately owned wildlife reserve has been geared towards rhino conservation since 1970. It plays a major role in the protection and breeding of black rhinos, but it also houses the largest population of white and black rhinos.

OPPOSITE:

Hell's Gate gorge, Hell's Gate National Park, Kenya

A Masai guide leads the way through Hell's Gate. The gorge runs through the heart of the park, which is surrounded by rusty-hued rock walls. It was named after a narrow break in the cliffs that was once a tributary of a prehistoric lake.

RIGHT TOP:

A flock of flamingos, Lake Bogoria National Reserve, Kenya

Lake Bogoria is a saline, alkaline lake located in the Great Rift Valley. It is home to one of the world's largest populations of lesser flamingos, the smaller species of the bird.

RIGHT BOTTOM:

Hippopotamuses, Lake Naivasha, Kenya

Lake Naivasha is home to a large population of hippos. Although docile looking, they are considered to be one of the most dangerous animals due to their aggressive and unpredictable nature.

FAR RIGHT:

Lake Naivasha, Kenya

Pelicans and numerous other bird species live beside the freshwater lake outside Naivasha town, which lies within the Rift Valley basin. The name Naivasha comes from the Masai word 'Naii'posha' meaning 'rough waters' due to the sudden storms that can occur.

ABOVE:

White sandy beach, Mombasa, Kenya
Known as 'the white and blue city' for its white sandy beaches and turquoise waters, Mombasa is the oldest city in Kenya. Given its strategic coastal location, it has been invaded many times during its history including by the Arabs and the British.

RIGHT:

Baghali Shah Mosque, Mackinnon Road town, Kenya
This mosque houses the tomb of Seyyid Baghali, a Punjabi Muslim foreman who worked on the Mombasa-Nairobi railway. Travellers began to attribute their safe journeys to visiting his grave, over which a mosque was later built.

**Old Town street life,
Mombasa, Kenya**
One of the yellow tuk-
tuks passes through the
characteristically narrow
streets of Old Town
Mombasa. Many tuk-tuk
drivers are now switching
to electric power.

**Market produce, Mombasa
Old town, Kenya**
The majority of outdoor
markets are on Mombasa
Island. They are a sensory
overload of people, smells and
noisy bartering. All kinds of
produce can be found here
from spices to dried pulses.

RIGHT:

Port of Mombasa, Mombasa, Kenya

The only international seaport in Kenya and the biggest port in East Africa, Mombasa Port can be traced back to a time when Arabian dhows (boats) arrived at the Old Port, on the north side of the island.

OPPOSITE:

Jain Temple, Mombasa, Kenya

Built in 1963 and located just outside the old town, this ornately decorated white marble structure is adorned with statues, gold spires and silver doors. It was the first of its kind to be built outside the Asian continent.

OVERLEAF:

Traditional Masai village, Arusha, Tanzania

The Masai live close to many of the African game parks in mud-dung houses. The nomadic Masai of the Great Rift Valley are traditionally pastoralist and have resisted attempts by the Kenyan and Tanzanian governments to become more sedentary.

LEFT:
Maasai women
Two Maasai women in traditional dress are talking to each other against the wall of a traditional house somewhere in Tanzania.

BELOW:
Maasai dance
Maasai men dancing and singing outdoors in traditional dress in Arusha, Tanzania.

Kilimanjaro at sunset
A view from Amboseli shows majestic Mount Kilimanjaro above the clouds at sunset.
A dormant volcano in Tanzania, Kilimanjaro is the highest mountain in Africa at 5895m (19,340ft). It is a popular hiking and climbing destination for the adventurous.

Mount Kilimanjaro, Tanzania
Of the seven summits in the world, Kilimanjaro is considered to be the easiest for climbing, but many people don't make it to the top due to altitude sickness. Although it's a dormant volcano, it could erupt again. The last eruption was 360,000 years ago.

LEFT:

**African elephant,
Ngorongoro Crater,
Tanzania**

The Lerai Forest inside the
crater provides a stunning
refuge for 25,000 mammals as
well as a variety of birds. The
Ngoitokitok Spring is a major
water source in the crater
where many elephants gather.
The crater also has one of the
densest populations of lions.

OPPOSITE:

**Ngorongoro Crater floor,
Tanzania**

The Masai name for 'black
hole', Ngorongoro was once
a giant volcano. It erupted
three million years ago and
is the world's largest intact
caldera. Many believe that
prior to its eruption, it would
have been higher than Mount
Kilimanjaro.

FAR LEFT & LEFT ABOVE:
Stone Town, Zanzibar, Tanzania
The historic part of Zanzibar city, Stone Town was the former capital of Zanzibar Sultanate and the centre of the spice trade and slave trade in the 19th century. It's name comes from the reddish coral stone used in the buildings. The narrow maze-like streets make walking or cycling the best way to get around.

LEFT BOTTOM:
Darajani Market, Stone Town, Zanzibar, Tanzania
The oldest and most popular market in Zanzibar, Darajani is primarily a food market with fresh fish , spices and other produce. Zanzibar is famed for its cloves, said to be the best in the world.

Dar es Salaam, Tanzania
The largest city in Tanzania and East Africa, Dar es Salaam has a population of over six million people. It was the political capital of the country until 1974 when it moved to Dodoma. Dar es Salaam, meaning 'home of peace' in Arabic, was built in 1865 by Sultan Majid bin Said of Zanzibar.

LEFT:

Baby gorilla, Bwindi Impenetrable National Park (BINP,) Uganda

Located in south-west Uganda, the BINP is a sanctuary for half of the world's population of endangered mountain gorillas. Due to its elevation, the forest has some of the richest fauna in East Africa.

RIGHT:

Lake Kivu, Rwanda

Kivu is surrounded by lush green mountains and has deep emerald freshwaters. A local delicacy is the sambaza fish. Fishermen catch them at night while singing traditional songs, hence they are known as the 'singing fishermen of Lake Kivu'.

RIGHT:
Fishermen, Lake Victoria
The largest lake in Africa and the largest tropical lake in the world, Lake Victoria runs across three countries. Also known as Victoria Nyanza, it has multiple names in different languages, but was renamed after Queen Victoria by a British explorer.

OPPOSITE:
Lake Nyasa
Nyasa is one of the Great African Lakes. It lies within Mozambique and Tanzania but mainly in Malawi. It's home to more species of fish than any other lake in the world. Nile crocodiles, hippos, monkeys and African fish eagles are found in and around the lake.

Southern Africa

Southern Africa is an anomaly from much of the continent with its plethora of natural wonders, wildlife and larger-than-life sites. These vary from the mesmerizing red dunes of Namibia and the mighty Zambezi River that cuts across much of the region to the Avenue of the Baobabs – famed for its centuries-old grove of striking trees – in western Madagascar. The diverse landscapes encompass desert, mountains, great plains and stunning coastlines. Dive into the clear waters of Bazaruto Island in Mozambique whose coral reefs are home to whales and more than 200 species of fish. Take in the extraordinary site of Victoria Falls, one of the world's largest waterfalls that is home to a unique array of plants and animals. Hang out with the lemurs of Madagascar or witness the zebra and other wildlife migrations in Botswana when the Okavango Delta swells to three times its size. Wander Madagascar's Nosy Boraha, once a popular base for pirates, now an idyllic whale-watching and beach island. You might prefer to peel back the layers of history in Namibia's abandoned mining town or in South Africa's Soweto to learn about its fight against apartheid. Or you can simply admire the vibrant houses of Cape Town's Bo-Kaap district and sip fine wines in the vineyards of Constantia Valley. Southern Africa rarely disappoints visitors.

OPPOSITE:
Elephant with young baby, Mana Pools National Park, Zimbabwe
'Mana' means pools in Shona, and refers to the four large pools inland from the river that form after the rainy season, drawing many animals in search of water. It is one of Africa's most popular game-viewing parks, particularly for elephants and lions.

RIGHT & OVERLEAF LEFT:
Victoria Falls, Zambia and Zimbabwe
One of the world's largest falls fed by the Zambezi River, this awe-inspiring waterfall provides habitat to several unique species of plants and animals. Evocatively known as Mosi-oa-Tunya ('the smoke that thunders') in the Lozi language or Shungu na mutitima ('boiling water') in Tonga, it was renamed Victoria Falls in 1855.

Zoa Falls, Mount Mulanje, Malawi

Zoa Falls is fed by the Ruo River that runs from Mulanje Mountain and empties into Shire River. The water drops off a 30-m (98ft) high cliff creating a fall similar to the splendour of Victoria Falls.

OPPOSITE:
Zambezi River
The fourth-longest river in Africa, the Zambezi is the largest
flowing river into the Indian Ocean from Africa. Its flows
through Angola, Namibia, Botswana, Zambia, Zimbabwe and
then Mozambique where it enters the Indian Ocean.

ABOVE:
**Elephants crossing the Zambezi River, Lower Zambezi
National Park, Zambia**
Before it became a national park in 1983, this area was the
private game reserve of Zambia's president. It remains one
of the few pristine wilderness areas in Africa.

Beach on Bazaruto Island, Mozambique
Bazaruto Island is the largest of the six islands that form the archipelago in Bazaruto National Park. The islands are revered for their unspoilt beauty and diverse eco-systems. The coral reefs are home to whales, dolphins and more than 200 species of fish.

RIGHT:

San Antonio Church, Mozambique Island, Mozambique

Before 1898 the island was the capital of Portuguese East Africa and a trading post en route to India. Pottery found on the island indicates it was established around the 14th century. The colonial church sits on the southern end overlooking the fishing port.

OPPOSITE:

Fort São Sebastião, Mozambique Island, Mozambique

This is the oldest and most complete fort still standing in Africa. The Portuguese started construction in 1558 and it took 62 years to complete. It has withstood many conquests and efforts to destroy it by the Dutch, British and Omanis.

ABOVE:
Statue of Samora Machel, Maputo, Mozambique
The bronze statue of Samora Machel, a revolutionary and the first President of Mozambique, is located in Independence Square. It was designed and made in North Korea. Although impressive, it is said to bear little resemblance to Samora.

OPPOSITE:
Tofo beach, Mozambique
Tofo is a small town in south-east Mozambique. Once a small fishing village, today it attracts many visitors who come for its pristine beaches and the chance to see the manta rays and whale sharks that live in these waters.

RIGHT:

Avenue of the Baobabs, Madagascar

Also known as 'Alley of the Baobabs', the baobab trees lining this dirt road in western Madagascar are up to 2800 years old. They are a striking visual reminder of the once dense tropical forests in Madagascar.

OPPOSITE:

Nosy Boraha, Madagascar

Previously known as Sainte-Marie, this was a popular base for pirates between the 17th and 18th centuries. Today the island is known for whale-watching and its idyllic beaches. Free from sharks, the island's lagoon is teeming with underwater life and is a popular diving site in the Indian Ocean.

LEFT:

Lemur, Madagascar
Lemurs are unique to the island and display a range of interesting characteristics such as their whale-like singing. Since Madagascar was isolated from evolutionary changes, the lemurs have developed with very little competition. There are over 110 different species of lemurs in Madagascar.

RIGHT:

Tsingy de Bemaraha Strict Nature Reserve, Madagascar
These needle-shaped limestone rock formations can cut through equipment and flesh, making them dangerous to cross. 'Tsingy' is a local word for 'the place where one cannot walk barefoot'. The reserve houses protected mangrove forests, wild birds and lemurs.

RIGHT:

Rainforest jungle, Masoala National Park, Madagascar
This is the largest and most biodiverse of Madagascar's protected areas. Within the park is a stunning array of landscapes and microclimates that sustain some of the rarest plants and animals, which can only be found here.

OPPOSITE TOP:

Panther chameleon, Madagascar
Madagascar is home to half of the world's 150 species of chameleons. The panther chameleon can grow up to 51cm (20in) long. It has a very long tongue that can rapidly extend to catch prey.

OPPOSITE BOTTOM:

Giant leaf-tail gecko, Nosy Mangabe Special Reserve, Madagascar
A giant leaf-tail gecko opens its mouth to show its bright red tongue as defence. This nocturnal gecko is native to Madagascar.

Grey heron and Egyptian geese at sunset, Lake Kariba, Matusadona National Park, Zimbabwe
Kariba is the fourth-largest artificial lake in the world. During the filling of the dam between 1958 and 1963, the water was rich in nutrients that created a thick layer of fertile soil, resulting in a vibrant lake ecology.

Great Zimbabwe Ruins, Zimbabwe

The largest collection of ruins in sub-Saharan Africa, Great Zimbabwe was built between the 11th and 15th centuries and was home to cattle-herding people. There are similar ruins known as zimbabwes that extend to Mozambique, but were pillaged by Europeans in the 19th century.

African leopard, South Luangwa National Park, Zambia

Often thought of as the most alluring of all of Africa's cats, the elusive leopard is easier to come across in Zambia's South Luangwa Park, where night safaris are offered. Hunting the prized feline is banned in Zambia.

Kubu Island, Botswana
A dry granite rock island, Kubu – known locally as Lekhubu – is located in the Makgadikgadi Pan, one of the world's largest salt flats. The entire island is a national monument and is considered a sacred site by the Khoikhoi people. A glorious starry night sky above a group of baobab trees accentuates the unique landscape.

RIGHT:

Hippopotamus, Moremi Game Reserve, Okavango Delta, Botswana

A hippopotamus yawns in the Moremi Game Reserve. The first reserve in Africa established by locals in 1963, it was named after Chief Moremi III of the Batawana people. Although not one of the largest parks, nearly 500 species of birds thrive here.

FAR RIGHT:

Baines Baobabs, Nxai Pan National Park, Botswana

Named after the painter and explorer Thomas Baines in 1862, these baobab trees are also known as the Sleeping Sisters. They are located in the large Nxai salt pan. Given the endless plains surrounding the baobabs, they are said to look like an island.

**Boat trip at sunset,
Okavango Delta, Botswana**
A *mokoro* is a traditional
canoe-like boat commonly
used in the Okavango Delta
as a mode of transport, and
for safaris.

**Okavango Delta (Okavango
Grassland), Botswana**
The largest inland delta in the
world, the Okavango appears
during the seasonal flooding
that peaks in July and August.
The swampy delta swells to
three times its size, attracting
animals from all around.

LEFT:

Epupa Falls (Monte Negro Falls), Namibia/Angola
Fed by the Cunene River on the border of Angola and
Namibia, this series of large waterfalls is called 'Epupa' – the
Herero (a Namibian tribe) word for foam.

ABOVE:

Natural canyon, Namib Desert, Angola
One of the oldest deserts in the world, with some of the driest
regions, it stretches for more than 1900km (1200mi) along the
Atlantic coasts of Angola, Namibia, and South Africa.

LEFT:

Fish River Canyon, Namibia
The largest canyon in Africa, and the second largest in the world, Fish River features a massive ravine. It is one of the more popular hiking trails in southern Africa.

ABOVE:

Quiver tree, Fish River Canyon National Park, Namibia
The quiver tree is related to the Aloe family. It's widely believed that the tree brings good luck to anyone who nurtures it. They grow in the semi-desert and can reach 5m (16ft) high.

Kolmanskop, Namibia
German miners settled in
Kolmanskop in 1908 after
a diamond had been found
and it became a rich mining
village. Wealthy miners
built the village in a German
architectural style; however,
by the early 1920s, there were
fewer diamonds and by 1956,
Kolmanskop was abandoned.

**Seal Colony, Cape Cross,
Namibia**
Home to one of the largest
colonies of cape fur seals
in the world, Cape Cross
is where the first European
explorer set foot on the
Namibian coast in 1486. Cape
Cross is one of two sites in
Namibia where a legal culling
of seals to protect fish stocks
takes place.

OPPOSITE:
Sossusvlei, Namib-Naukluft National Park, Namibia
Massive red sand dunes surrounding a white salt and clay pan
create a magnificent landscape. Unsurprisingly, this is one of
the country's biggest attractions. Sossusvlei means 'dead-end
marsh' and this is where the dunes come together to stop the
Tsauchab River from flowing further.

ABOVE:
**Dead camel thorn trees, Deadvlei, Namib-Naukluft
National Park, Namibia**
The white clay pan formed after rainfall when the Tsauchab
River flooded, allowing camel thorn trees to grow. Later,
drought hit and sand dunes took over, blocking the river and
killing the trees some 700 years ago.

ALL PHOTOGRAPHS:

Spitzkoppe, Namibia
The Spitzkoppe is one of
the most photographed
mountain ranges in Namibia
and is more than 700 million
years old. Its granite peaks
jut out 700m (2296ft) from
its surroundings. Given its
distinctive form, it can be
seen from a large distance.
The photograph opposite
shows the famous Rock Arch
at Spitzkoppe.

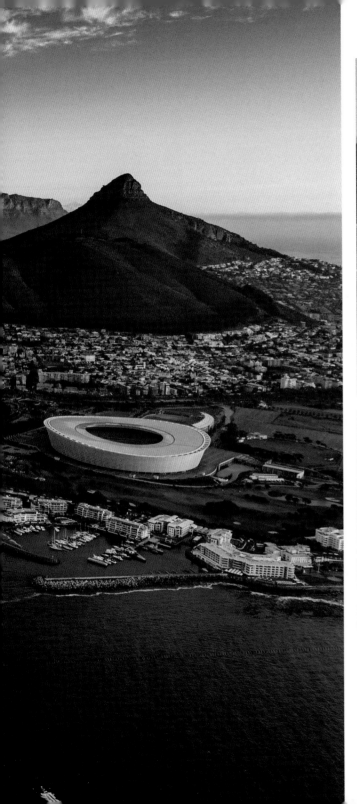

LEFT TOP:

Cape Town Harbour, South Africa

The harbour lies in the shadow of Table Mountain. Cape Town sits at nearly the most southern tip of Africa.

LEFT BOTTOM:

Bo-Kaap, Cape Town, South Africa

Bo-Kaap is known for its cobblestone streets and brightly coloured buildings. The latter hark back to the 1830s when, following the abolition of slavery, newly liberated slaves painted their homes with bright colours to express their freedom as homeowners.

FAR LEFT:

Cape Town, South Africa

One of South Africa's three capital cities, Cape Town is is the oldest. Founded by the Dutch East India Company, it was the first permanent European settlement in South Africa. Table Mountain, Devil's Peak and Lion's Head form a mountainous backdrop that encloses the central area of Cape Town.

Tugela River leading to the Amphitheatre, Drakensberg, South Africa
The Tugela River flows through the Drakensberg range before cascading down a series of waterfalls and through the Tugela Gorge. In the background lies the Amphitheatre, regarded as one of the most impressive cliff faces in the world.

ALL PHOTOGRAPHS:
Soweto, Johannesburg, South Africa

Soweto was created in the 1930s when the white government began to segregate blacks and whites, and blacks were moved away from Johannesburg to create black 'townships'. Soweto grew from a shanty town to become the largest black city in South Africa. Notable residents include former President Nelson Mandela. Following the uprising in 1976 by students protesting the introduction of the Afrikaans language as the medium of teaching in black schools, the deadly government crackdown shone an international light on the township and its fight for freedom. Many poor Sowetans continue to live in basic sheds and shacks.

LEFT:
Robben Island, South Africa
An island in Table Bay, it was fortified and used as a prison from the late 17th century until 1996. Political activist Nelson Mandela was imprisoned here for 18 years along with other political prisoners who fought the apartheid regime.

BELOW:
African penguins, Boulders Penguin Colony, Cape Town
Boulders has become famous for its thriving colony of African penguins. In 1982, just two breeding pairs were brought in, and since then, the colony has grown to about 2200.

BELOW:
Bloukrans Bridge, South Africa
Bloukrans Bridge, near Nature's Valley in Western Cape, has been the location of the world's highest commercial bungee jump since 1997. Jumps take place from the arch bridge that stands 216m (708ft) above Bloukrans River.

OPPOSITE:
Vineyards, Constantia Valley, South Africa
Constantia is one of the oldest suburbs of Cape Town and is renowned for wine from the valley vineyards. The oldest wine estate was established in 1685 by Simon van der Stel, the first governor of the Dutch Cape Colony.

ABOVE:

Buffalo at the source, Kruger National Park, South Africa
Many African (Cape) buffalo can be seen at Kruger National
Park, the largest game reserve in the world. They are usually
found in herds, often in their hundreds.

OPPOSITE:

Lioness and her cub, Kruger National Park, South Africa
Kruger is home to a large African lion population. Lions prey
mostly on large animals such as zebra and wildebeest. The
hunting is usually left to the lioness of the pride.

Picture Credits